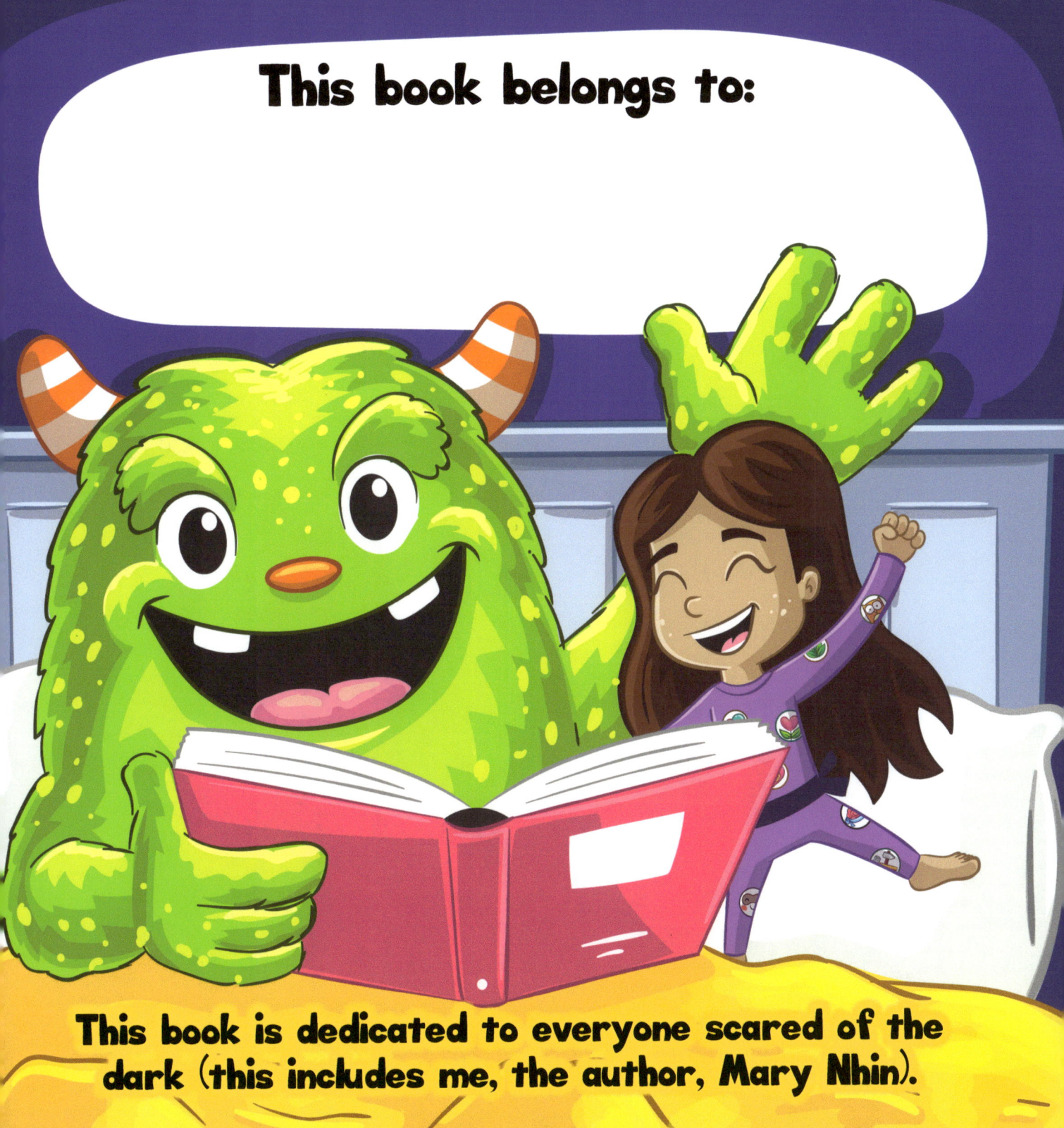

Copyright © 2024 Grow Grit Press LLC. All rights reserved. No part of this book may be reproduced in any form without permission in writing from the publisher. Please send bulk order requests to info@ninjalifehacks.tv

Paperback ISBN: 978-1-63731-954-3
Hardcover ISBN: 978-1-63731-956-7
eBook ISBN: 978-1-63731-955-0

Printed and bound in the USA.
NinjaLifeHacks.tv

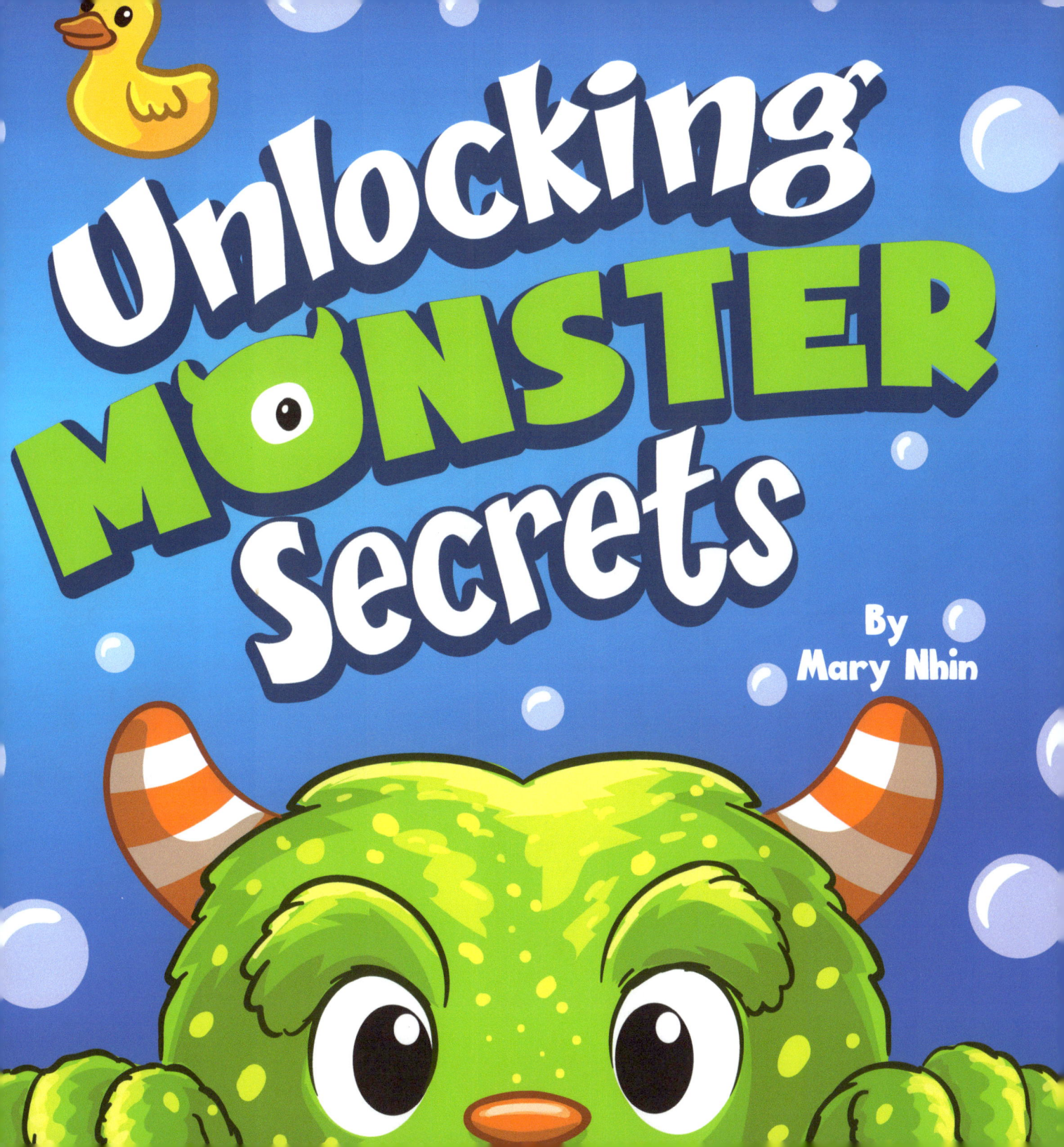

There's a beast in my wardrobe,
With fuzzy fur, sharp claws, and wild hair.
Tonight I plan to meet him,
His **LAIR** is right over there!

"It's just a rubber duck," I giggle,
As he backs away in fright.
A monster scared of yellow DUCKS—
Now, isn't that a sight?

"Why do you fear this tiny thing?"
I ask as he takes a peek.
"It's weird and it squeaks so loud,
Just **TERRIFIES** me every week!"

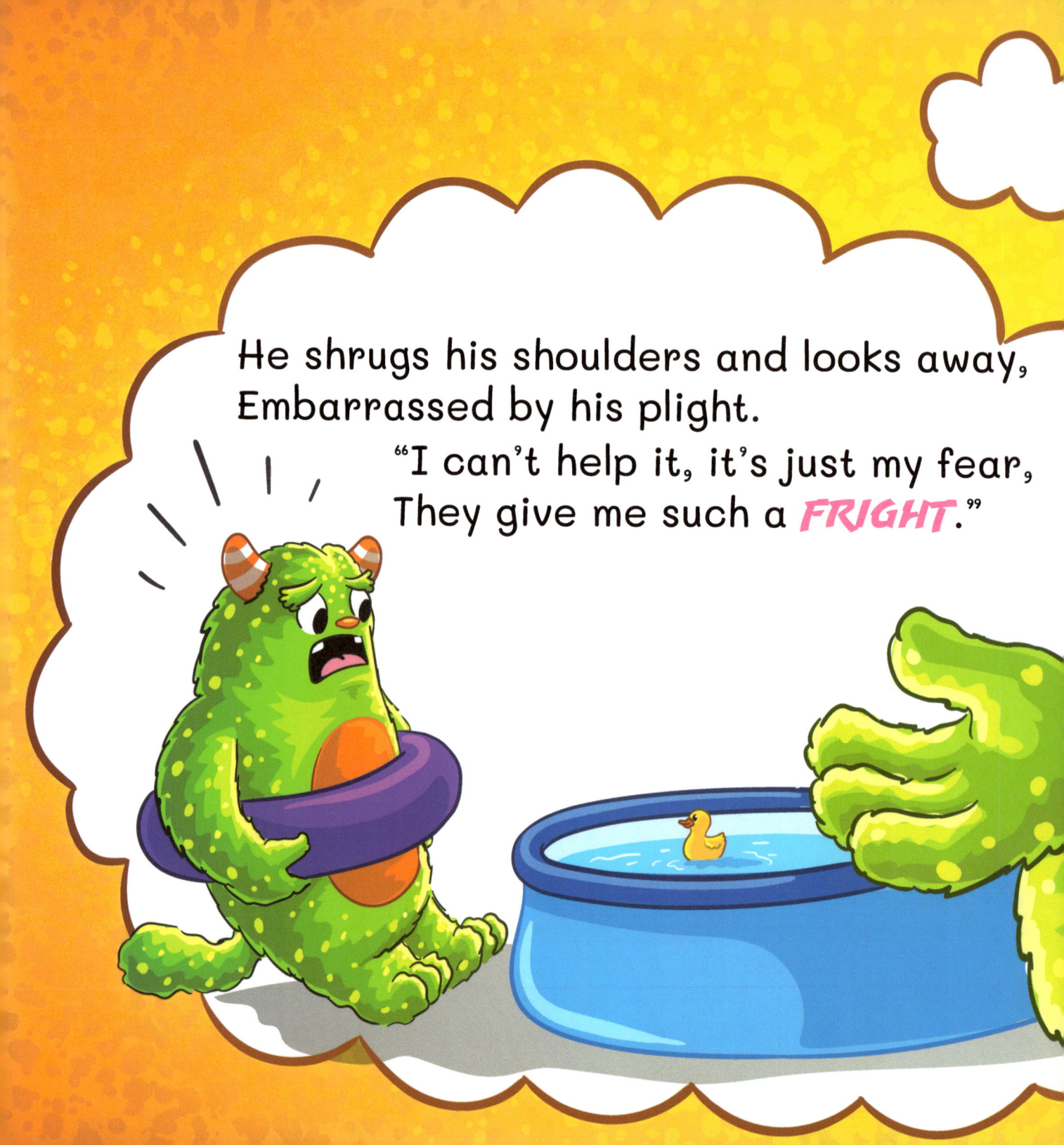

He shrugs his shoulders and looks away,
Embarrassed by his plight.
"I can't help it, it's just my fear,
They give me such a **FRIGHT**."

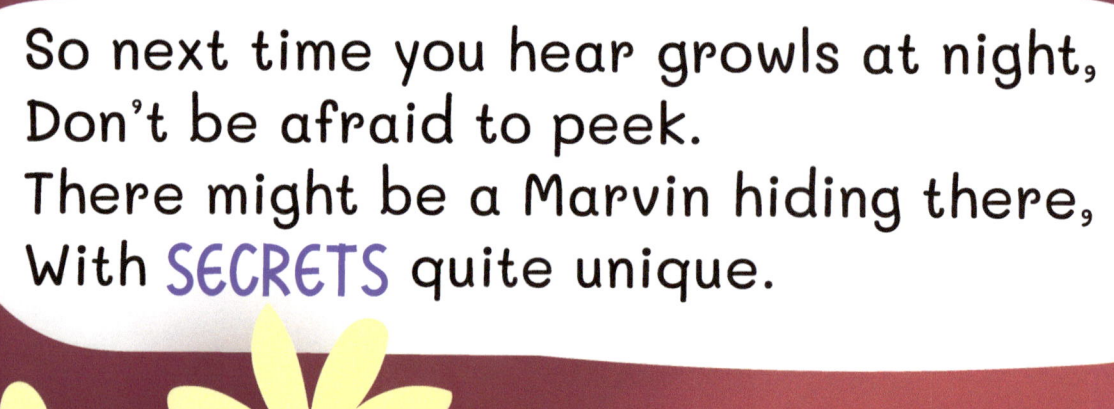

So next time you hear growls at night,
Don't be afraid to peek.
There might be a Marvin hiding there,
With SECRETS quite unique.

For monsters big and ninjas small,
All have fears to fight.
And with a **friend** to help them through,
They'll find they're quite alright!

I love to hear from my readers. Email me your feedback or thoughts on what my next story should be at info@ninjalifehacks.tv

Yours truly, Mary

 @marynhin   @GrowGrit
#NinjaLifeHacks

 Mary Nhin   Ninja Life Hacks

 Ninja Life Hacks

 @officialninjalifehacks

www.ingramcontent.com/pod-product-compliance
Lightning Source LLC
Chambersburg PA
CBHW041711160426
43209CB00018B/1805